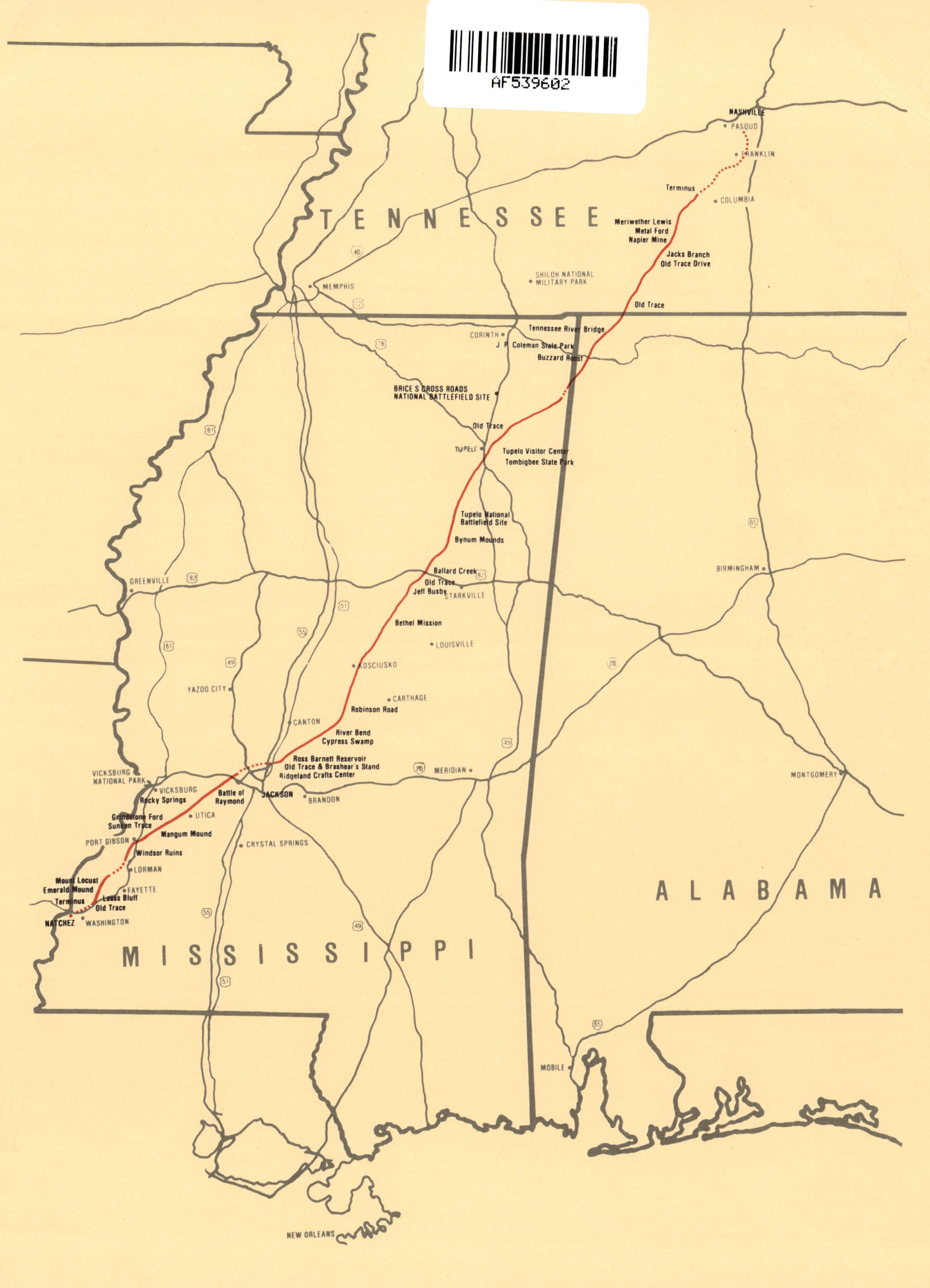
TENNESSEE
MISSISSIPPI
ALABAMA
NASHVILLE
PASQUO
FRANKLIN
Terminus
COLUMBIA
Meriwether Lewis
Metal Ford
Napier Mine
Jacks Branch
Old Trace Drive
SHILOH NATIONAL MILITARY PARK
MEMPHIS
40
72
Old Trace
Tennessee River Bridge
CORINTH
J P Coleman State Park
Buzzard Roost
78
BRICE S CROSS ROADS NATIONAL BATTLEFIELD SITE
Old Trace
61
TUPELO
Tupelo Visitor Center
Tombigbee State Park
Tupelo National Battlefield Site
Bynum Mounds
65
Ballard Creek
82
Old Trace
Jeff Busby
STARKVILLE
GREENVILLE
82
BIRMINGHAM
51
55
Bethel Mission
61
LOUISVILLE
49
KOSCIUSKO
20
YAZOO CITY
CARTHAGE
Robinson Road
CANTON
River Bend
Cypress Swamp
45
Ross Barnett Reservoir
Old Trace & Brashear's Stand
Ridgeland Crafts Center
80
MERIDIAN
MONTGOMERY
VICKSBURG NATIONAL PARK
VICKSBURG
Rocky Springs
Battle of Raymond
JACKSON
BRANDON
Grindstone Ford
Sunken Trace
UTICA
PORT GIBSON
Mangum Mound
CRYSTAL SPRINGS
Windsor Ruins
LORMAN
Mount Locust
Emerald Mound
FAYETTE
Terminus
Loess Bluff
Old Trace
NATCHEZ
WASHINGTON
55
49
51
65
MOBILE
NEW ORLEANS

The Natchez Trace

William,
Welcome to Mississippi! We hope this is the first of many trips!
Steve

Biloxi
6/4/86

The NATCHEZ TRACE

Photographs by
HAROLD YOUNG
With text by Patti Carr Black

UNIVERSITY PRESS OF MISSISSIPPI
Jackson

The University Press of Mississippi gratefully acknowledges the following agencies for permission to publish photographs:

The Natchez Trace Parkway, for the photographs on pages 5, 6, 8, 9, 12, 13, 16, 17.

The Tennessee State Library and Archives, for the photograph of Andrew Jackson on page 8.

The University Press of Mississippi also thanks Ray Claycomb, Assistant Chief Park Interpreter, and other members of the staff of the Natchez Trace Parkway, for their assistance.

Printed in Japan

Library of Congress Cataloging in Publication Data

Young, Harold.
The Natchez Trace.

1. Natchez Trace—Description and travel—Views.
I. Black, Patti Carr. II. Title
F217.N37Y68 1985 976.2 84-7219
ISBN 0-87805-226-7

Introduction

By the time President Thomas Jefferson in 1806 ordered the Natchez road to be "12 feet in width and made passable for a wagon," the trail had already played a dramatic role on America's turbulent frontier. Along river ridges, through canebrakes, swamps, and forests, the trail carried many of the gallant *dramatis personae* of the westward movement.

French explorers tramping through the Deep South in the eighteenth century had found a network of paths, perhaps first beaten down by herds of buffalo, used by Indians as trails linking villages and tribes. (The old French word for such trails was *trace,* which meant a line of footprints or animal tracks.) These paths, when joined together, led northeasterly from the Natchez Indian set-

Excavation of the Bynum Mounds near Houston, Mississippi, in 1948 uncovered some of the secrets of the prehistoric peoples who traveled the Trace.

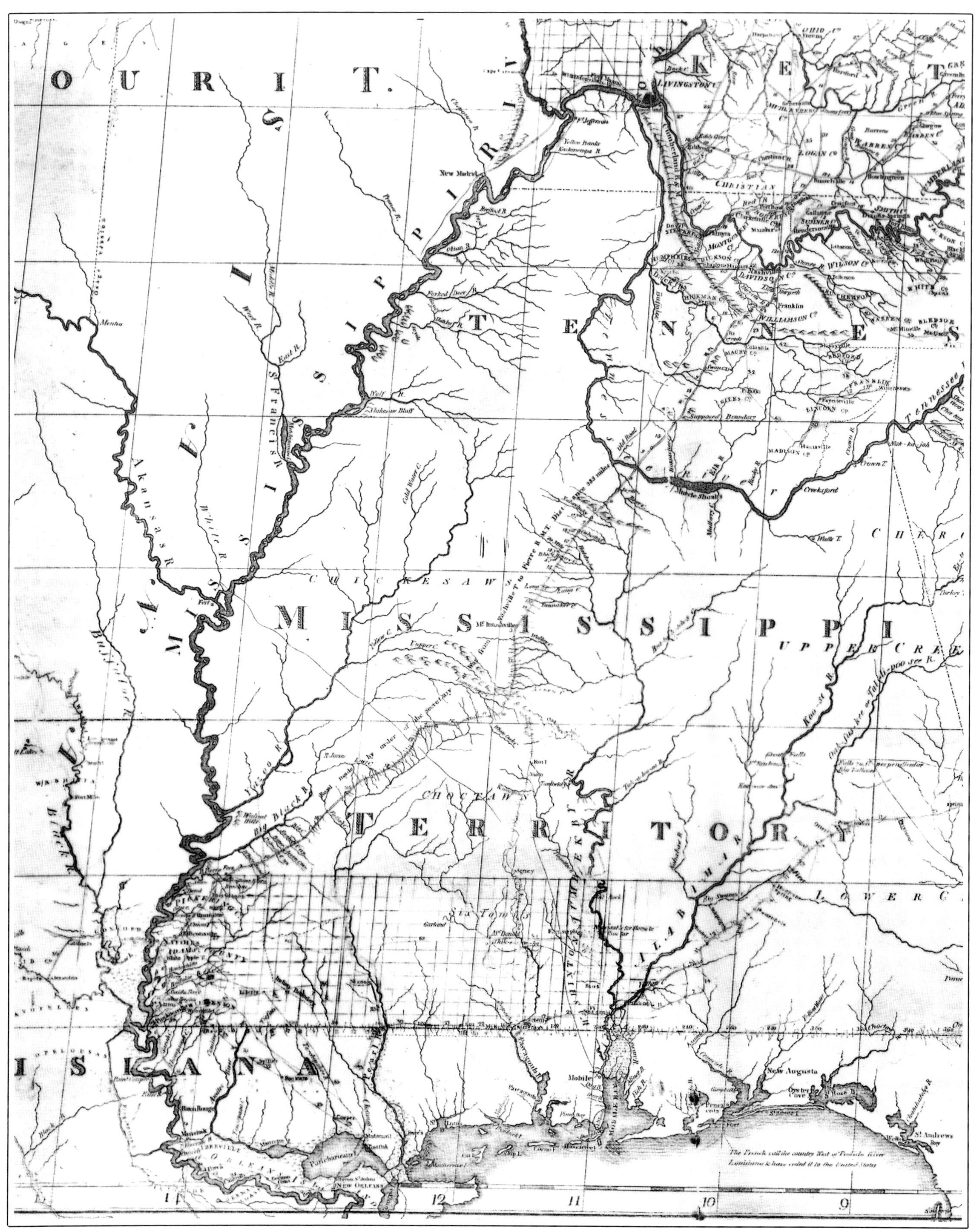

Early nineteenth century map showing Natchez Trace when it was used as a post road

tlements on the Mississippi River through Choctaw, Chickasaw, and probably Cherokee lands, to present-day Nashville, Tennessee.

The French, who first settled on the Gulf Coast, moved up the Mississippi River and set up a post at Natchez in 1716, primarily for trading with the Indians. French trappers, traders, and missionaries began using "the path through the Choctaw Nation," and "the Chickasaw trace" to travel to and from the interior of Indian country. As successive groups of white settlers moved in and used the trails for commercial and military activities, they became increasingly important. France ceded the Natchez area to Great Britain in 1763 and there followed a great influx of English-speaking settlers, who came part way over the old Indian paths, and who were to give Natchez and Mississippi their dominant culture for centuries to come. Then the Spanish came, taking over the Natchez territory during the American Revolution and annexing it to the Colony of Louisiana. As Spain encouraged immigration, American settlers continued to push inland from the older settlements on the Atlantic seaboard. Many settled at the northern end of the Trace at Nashville, while some pushed further southwest to the Natchez area. In 1798, the United States gained control of the area and created the Mississippi Territory with Natchez as its capital.

Because Natchez had strategic military, diplomatic, and economic significance to the country, an adequate means of communication with Washington was needed. Congress established a postal route on the Trace in 1800 even though the postmaster general described it as "no other than an Indian footpath very devious and narrow." In 1801 the Chickasaw and Choctaw nations granted permission to the United States government to open the route across their tribal lands. Under the Secretary of War, desultory attempts were made to clear out the path and bridge some of the creeks and swamps for travelers already using the Trace. It was the new lands of the Louisiana Purchase that brought more and more traffic to the been made practicable, the distance from Nashville to Natchez will be four hundred and fifty miles — on the present travelled route the distance is five hundred. This route may be divided into four parts —

1st From Natchez to Grindstone ford, a distance of 70 miles. This part is in decent order and requires no expenditure.

2ndly. From Grindstoneford about 40 miles towards the Chickasaw Towns, at or near Snake Creek. This part of the road has been cut by the Military and cleared off for a very considerable width, much greater than is necessary for the public service, but some expenditure will be necessary to clear off the under bushes and to make the passage of the waters convenient & secure.

3rd. From Snake Creek, past the Chickasaw Towns, to, or near Buffaloe Creek, 40 miles to the South of the river Tennessee — the distance of this portion of the route is estimated at 186 miles. This portion of the route is entirely in a wilderness state —

4thly, from Buffaloe Creek to the Tenessee river 40 miles and from thence to Nashville 114 miles, making in the whole the distance of 154. This part of the route has also been cut out by the Military, but requires an expenditure to remove the under growth and to facilitate the passage over the waters —

In order to put the whole route into a state of repair, I take the liberty to submit the following plan to your consideration —

That the route be divided into three parts. 1st From Nashville to Buffaloe Creek the distance of 154 miles. 2ndly From Buffaloe Creek to Snake Creek 186 miles - where a new road is to be made. 3d. From Snake Creek to Grindstone ford - distance 40 miles. And to issue an advertisement from this office, inviting bidders to send in their proposals to the General Post Office by the first day of December next

Letter from Postmaster General Gideon Granger to President Thomas Jefferson, requesting repairs on the post road between Nashville and Natchez

trail and prompted Congress to appropriate funds for improvements in 1806.

In the meantime, up and down the Trace, the great movement of frontier people continued: settlers, traders, circuit-riding preachers, soldiers, government officials, politicians, post riders, backwoodsmen, and boatmen. A few traveled on horseback, most on foot in groups with pack horses. Pushmataha and Tecumseh, famous Indian chiefs; Louis LeFleur, French trader; the Marquis de LaFayette, Henry Clay, the boy Jefferson Davis, Jim Bowie, and other legendary figures had business up and down the Trace. Captain Meriwether Lewis of Lewis and Clark fame lost his life on the Trace when he was mysteriously shot at Grinder's Inn in 1809, and Aaron Burr traveled over part of the Trace for his treason hearing at Washington, Mississippi. Naturalists John James Audubon and Alexander Wilson sketched bird life in the wilderness of the Trace, and itinerant evangelists like Lorenzo Dow, "the crazy preacher," followed their human flocks westward.

Meriwether Lewis

One of the most famous travelers on the Trace was Andrew Jackson, who began making trips up and down the Trace after the Revolutionary War, negotiating with the Spanish, trading in slaves, dealing with Indian problems. As a young lawyer, he traveled the road to court Rachel Donelson Robards, whom he married a half mile off the Trace at the plantation "Springfield" near Fayette. When the United States declared war on England in 1812, Andrew Jackson moved his Tennessee militia of more than two thousand men down river toward New Orleans, stopping to camp in Adams County, at Washington. It was on the march home up the Trace in early 1813 that Jackson earned his nickname "Old Hickory." At the end of that war, after a brilliant victory over the British at the Battle of New Orleans, Andrew Jackson with his wife and small son and their entourage took the Trace home to fame and ultimately the presidency.

Andrew Jackson

Perhaps the most colorful of the Trace travelers were the fabled boatmen called "Kaintucks," who achieved legendary fame in the tales of Mike Fink, "half alligator and half horse." When a treaty with Spain opened the Mississippi River to navigation in 1795, the boatmen, who were initially farmers, floated the farm products of the Ohio Valley downstream to Natchez and New Orleans to be shipped to Europe or the eastern United States. After the boatmen reached Natchez or New Orleans and delivered their cargoes, they returned home through the countryside because the steamboat had not yet been invented and poling up river against the current was tedious and long. These men came from many different states, as did their cargoes, but down south they were all called "Kaintucks," a name synonymous with rough-and-rowdy. Andrew Jackson is quoted as saying, "I never met a Kaintuck who did not have a rifle, a pack of cards, and a bottle of whiskey."

From mid-February to July of each year, the Ohio and Mississippi rivers were filled with barges, flatboats, and keel boats loaded down with flour, pork, tobacco, hemp, and iron, floating south. As these products of the Ohio Valley, Illinois country, and the Natchez district were shipped down the Mississippi River, gold and silver from New Orleans flowed up the Natchez Trace as payment. It has been determined that by 1810, ten thousand men made their way down river in this trade each season. They usually began their journey home by knocking apart their great rafts, selling them for lumber, and

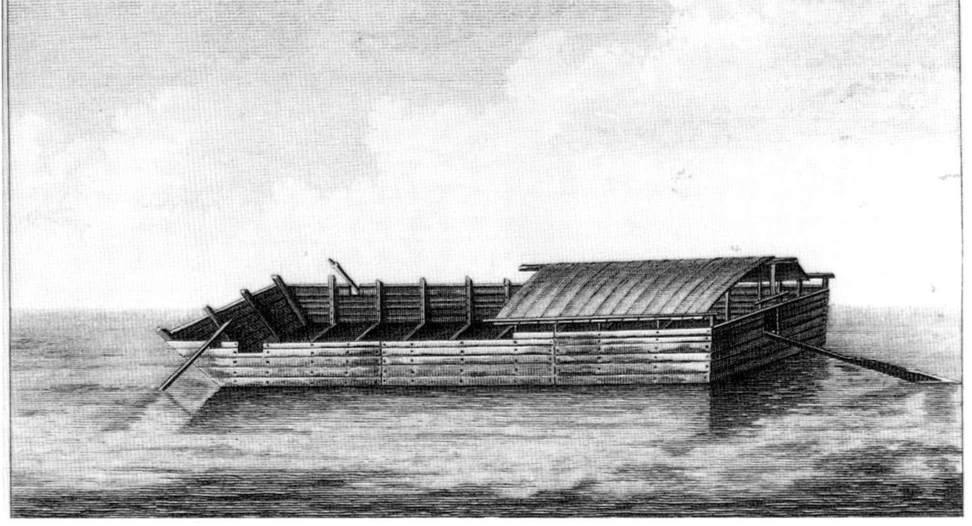

Sketch of a flat bottom boat such as the "Kaintucks" used to float Ohio Valley farm products down the Mississippi River to Natchez.

heading for Natchez-Under-the-Hill, where gambling, brothels, dock-side musicians, fist-fights, and Indians selling ponies provided a lively time, and perhaps memories for the rough trip ahead.

Another famous group on the Trace were the outlaws. The movement of settlers coming down the Trace and the boatmen going up the Trace with pouches of silver from the ports of New Orleans drew robbers like a magnet. The Mason gang, led by Revolutionary War veteran Samuel Mason, was the most notorious. The gang, which included Mason's son John and Wiley "Little" Harp operated out of a canebreak near Vicksburg. They terrorized the Trace until Governor Claiborne put up a $2000 reward for the capture of Mason. His head was delivered to authorities in old Greenville by "Little" Harp in disguise, who in turn was recognized, tried, and hanged for his crime.

There were other dangers and discomforts along the Trace: steamy swamps, mosquitoes, accidents, illness, hunger, and the weather. From January to March the rains made the creeks and swamps along the road hazardous and almost impassable. One British journalist wrote of travelers having to swim through swamps and of plunging "up to the saddle-skirts in mire at every step. The bottom," he continued, "is stiff dry clay and horses sometimes stick so fast that they cannot be extricated, but are left to die."

The journey from Natchez to Nashville was a distance of some five hundred miles and required fifteen to twenty days to make the trip. Before setting off on the Trace in either direction travelers packed provisions for the trip. Along with corn whiskey and apple brandy, they took flour, bacon, dried beef, rice, coffee, sugar, and a small supply of roasted Indian corn ground to a powder for emergency ration. Experienced hunters could supplement provisions with turkey, deer, rabbit, and wild honey in the forest. Much attention was also given to clothing. Thick walking shoes were essential and travelers usually wore the protective hunter's costume of coarse brown overalls

Mr John McIntosh   June 27
Chickasaw Nation

Sir, The mail from Nashville to the Natchez after the first of July next is to be carried once a fortnight agreeably to the following Schedule:

Leave Nashville every other Sunday at 9 a.m.
Arrive at McIntoshes the next Friday by 8 p.m. .... 230 miles
Leave McIntoshes the next Sunday by 5 a.m.
Arrive at Natchez the next Saturday by 2 p.m. .. 270
500

Returning

Leave Natchez the next day Sunday by 5 a.m.
Arrive at McIntoshes the next Sunday by 8 a.m.
Leave McIntoshes the next day Monday by 5 a.m.
Arrive at Nashville the next Saturday by 5 p.m.

Mr Lyon has the contract from Nashville to McIntoshs & Mr Abijah Hunt the Post Master of the Natchez the other part of the route. From some delay Mr Hunt has not received the counterpart of the Contract for his part of the route & he may not have made provision for the conveyance of the mail — if this should be the case I wish you to forward the mail by Express to the Natchez for which you will be paid until Mr Hunt's riders are prepared to carry it agreeably to his contract.

I am I.H.

Letter to John McIntosh describing the mail schedule between Nashville and Natchez in the early 1800s.

and shirts. Accommodations along the Trace were as primitive as the road itself. The Chickasaw and Choctaw Nations had agreed that a wagon road could be cut through their land, but fearful of the white's incursions into their territory, they would not consent to the establishment of "stands" in Indian country until 1805. Even after that, these stands or inns were slow to materialize.

For the first seventy miles from Natchez north, the going was fairly easy. The Trace ran roughly parallel to the Mississippi River through flat country that was at least sparsely populated by white settlers and where a person might find shelter at a farm or an inn. One traveler in 1798 wrote of stopping at Grindstone Ford, near Port Gibson, where for twenty-five cents he had a meal of mush and milk and the privilege of sleeping on the floor in a room filled with saddles, baggage, lumber, and other travelers. Other inns along the settled section of the Trace were at Washington, Selsertown, Uniontown (now Mt. Locust), old Greenville, Port Gibson, and gradually all the way to the boundary of the Natchez District.

To the east stretched Indian country. The early Nashville-bound travelers passing through Choctaw country had only abandoned Indian campsites for accommodations. After about 1810, there were Brashear's Stand, Doak's Stand, French Camp (named for the nationality of Louis LeFleur, its founder and proprietor), and Pigeon Roost (run by David Folsom, part English and part Choc-

This section of the original Trace at Jack's Branch in Tennessee shows conditions on the Trace before it was paved.

taw and the first Choctaw chief elected by ballot). When the early traveler reached the Chickasaw lands, he could stop near the "big town" of the Chickasaw, where their wood huts, corn and tobacco fields, and orchards of peaches and apples afforded the well-known Chickasaw hospitality. After 1808, in the Chickasaw nation, there were the stands of James, Levi, and George Colbert, all chieftains and sons of William Colbert, a Scotsman, and his Chickasaw wife, and the stand of James Allen, who also married a Chickasaw, reported to be the daughter of William Colbert. There was also "Tockshish," a settlement started by John McIntosh, who had been sent to the Chickasaw Nation by the British government before the American Revolution and who stayed to live among the Indians. The use of the word "stand" can better be understood with an 1816 description by a circuit rider on the Trace: "The Indian hotels are made of small poles, just high enough for you to stand straight in, with a dirt floor, no bedding of any kind, except a bearskin, and not that in some huts."

Forty miles beyond the Chickasaw villages, the Trace crossed the Tennessee River where the ferry boat concession was operated by George Colbert, a powerful and influential leader in the Chickasaw Nation. Colbert is said to have grown quite wealthy operating the ferry, especially in 1815 when Andrew Jackson brought his army across at a reputed cost of $75,000. The seventy-five miles of road between the Tennessee River and the Duck River ridge, which was the Indian boundary line, were the most arduous part of the journey. Between the rivers was Grinder's Inn, where Meriwether Lewis died and is buried. Across Duck River the ferry and stand were operated by a close friend of Andrew Jackson's, the famous Indian scout John Gordon, who was awarded the land for his deeds against the Creek Indians. Once over Duck River the traveler was in Tennessee and hiking the last fifty miles through the mountains, where he again encountered white settlers. Finally arriving in Nashville, travelers could set out on well-defined roads in almost any direction.

For over two decades, this link between the two important and lively frontier towns was an essential national highway, providing the capital of the young nation with access to its new lands in the Old Southwest. Gradually, however, the great movement up and down the Trace subsided. Ironically, one of the last groups of immigrants to use the Trace were those who had first trampled it into a path. The Indians, exiled from their land, started their move to Oklahoma by going down the Trace to Walnut Hills (now Vicksburg), where they left the state of Mississippi forever.

The factors in the decline of the Trace were as important a part in the drama of American history as its origin and use had been. The catalytic factor was the invention of the steamboat in 1811. It took a few years to convince skeptics that the new way was a better way to ship merchandise, but no one could argue that the new boat was superior in ascending the river. By 1821 there were sixty-one steamboats operating on the Mississippi and Ohio rivers, and they offered a cheap escape from the vagaries and hardships of a journey on the Natchez Trace. The postal business was also captured by the steamboat, making the Trace less and less important in the nation's business. The steamboat dealt the final death knell to the Trace by making the water route from Mobile to New Orleans feasible and offering a new, shorter "southern route" from Washington to New Orleans through the south Atlantic states.

By the 1830s the great days of the Natchez Trace had come to an end, and eventually portions of its route became lost in grasslands and encroaching woods. For one hundred years the Trace went back to what it had been, a series of disjointed trails, used chiefly for local travel.

The comeback of the road is a modern and altogether different drama of politics. The Depression of the 1930s provided the impetus to put the pieces of the Trace back

Some portions of the original Trace, like this section in central Mississippi, became part of the county road system in Mississippi.

together. Franklin Delano Roosevelt's New Deal searched for projects that would create jobs and be useful to local governments. The Daughters of the American Revolution had been calling attention to the historic significance of the Trace since 1909 by erecting markers along the route. By 1934 their efforts had persuaded Mississippi Congressman Jeff Busby to introduce a resolution asking the Interior Department to make "a survey of the old Indian trail known as the Natchez Trace with a view to constructing a national road on the route to be known as the Natchez Trace Parkway." When Senator Hubert D. Stephens of Mississippi introduced an identical bill in the Senate, the Interior Department urged a presidential veto of the $50,000 survey. Had Roosevelt not needed the support of the chairman of the Senate Finance Committee, Pat Harrison of Mississippi, the resolution might never have passed. The survey was made, and in 1937 funds were allotted from the president's "emergency funds" for the construction of the parkway, which was to be a unit of the National Park Service.

Today the Natchez Trace Parkway roughly follows the old Natchez Trace, crossing and recrossing it through a protected area of deep woods, rolling hills, meadows, high ridges, and bottomlands. Although the parkway is still not completed, the projected length is 449 miles, with 313 stretching diagonally across Mississippi, 33 miles dog-earing the corner of Alabama, and the last 103 stretching into Tennessee. Approximately 19 million travel the Natchez Trace Parkway each year. Commercial vehicles are not allowed, and a fifty-miles-per-hour speed zone discourages the strictly-business motorist. Along the way,

The work of a park ranger in 1947, when the Natchez Trace Parkway was still under construction, was quite different from a ranger's job today.

the Park Service provides campgrounds, picnic tables, nature trails, historic markers, and exhibits that introduce the traveler to virtually all of the area's history. The traveler can explore archaelogical sites, an early inn, Indian sites, and Civil War battlefields and even walk on short sections of the original trace. For those interested only in its spectacular scenery, the Trace can be the glorious experience of a single day. Harold Young's photographs capture both of these possibilities, showing us the beauty and the enchantment of a trail that reveals an exciting moment of America's history at almost every turn.

Patti Carr Black

The Natchez Trace

Mississippi River, Natchez

Docked at Natchez-Under-the-Hill are
The Delta Queen *(built 1928) and* The Mississippi Queen *(built 1976),*
the only riverboats still plying the Mississippi River.

DELTA QUEEN
MISSISSIPPI QUEEN

Natchez-Under-the-Hill, once a colorful and lively district catering to flatboatmen, is being reconstructed today with restaurants and shops for tourists.

King's Tavern, one of the oldest structures in Mississippi, was already famous by 1800 as a stopping place for Kentucky boatmen.

Dunleith, in Natchez, was built around 1857, after the heyday of the Trace.

Family cemetery, north of Natchez

Jefferson College received the state's first educational charter in 1802. Located in Washington, the capital of the Mississippi Territory, the college grounds were the site of the first constitutional convention in 1817.

The original Natchez Trace leads into the woods along the roadway.

Near Highway 553 to Fayette

"Spanish Moss" on trees is typical of the lower Trace region. Not really a moss of Spanish origin, the flowering plant Tillandsia *hangs on trees but gets most of its nutrients from rainwater.*

Emerald Mound, built around 1300, is one of the largest ceremonial mounds in the United States. It covers nearly eight acres and measures 770 feet by 435 feet at the base.

Emerald Mound

Loess Bluff shows a deep deposit of topsoil (loess) blown into the area during the Ice Age.

Mount Locust, one of the first stands, or inns, on the Trace was restored by the National Park Service. Living history programs are presented there March through October.

Turpin Creek

According to tradition, Andrew Jackson married Rachel Donelson Robards at "Springfield," just off the Trace in Jefferson County, Mississippi, in 1791.

Coles Creek picnic area

An unfinished portion of the Trace routes travelers by the Old Country Store at Lorman, Mississippi.

Roadside flea market at Lorman, Mississippi

Spring wildflowers

Windsor, a plantation house erected 1859–60 near Port Gibson, was destroyed by fire in 1890. The property is now owned by the state and administered by the Department of Archives and History.

Port Gibson was the first town still extant to grow up along the Trace. One of the oldest houses in Port Gibson is the Englesing House, built in 1817.

Old sunken trace near Port Gibson

Barn near the site of Grindstone Ford on the eastern frontier of the Old Natchez District. Grindstone Ford was the jumping-off place into the wilderness of Indian country for the early traveler.

Near Mangum Mound, Claiborne County, Mississippi

The Mississippi Track Club has annual runs winter and summer on the Trace.

Dogwood along the Trace

Rocky Springs Methodist Church, built in 1837

Picnic area at Rocky Springs, Mississippi

Rocky Springs

Old Trace at Rocky Springs, Mississippi, the site of an early postal stop on the Trace and the campsite of General Grant's army in its march to Jackson and Vicksburg

Rocky Springs

Dupree Plantation near Utica. The house, sometimes called "Edgewood," was built around 1848 by Samuel Heard.

New farm technology produces roll bales.

All year round bicyclists use the section of the Trace between Washington and Clinton, where the terrain is extremely flat.

Mississippi Crafts Center, Ridgeland, operated by the Mississippi Craftsmen's Guild.

Near Ridgeland, Mississippi

Demonstrations of crafts by artisans are given throughout the year at the Mississippi Crafts Center at Ridgeland: (top left) Susan Ford, glassblower; (right) Susan Denson, Choctaw basketmaker; (bottom left) Ernest Henning, white oak basketmaker.

Split rail fence, near the site of Brashear's stand, advertised in 1806 as "a house of entertainment in the wilderness"

Ross Barnett Reservoir, constructed in 1959, parallels the parkway for eight miles.

On Ross Barnett Reservoir

Cypress Swamp, a nature trail for today's traveler, was a mosquito-laden, treacherous obstacle for early travelers.

A wooden foot bridge over Cypress Swamp is part of a trail leading through the abandoned channel of the Pearl River.

Cypress swamp

Near Kosciusko

South of Kosciusko, the town where the Natchez Trace Festival is staged each June.

Bethel Mission Church near French Camp is on the site of one of the thirteen missions to the Choctaws established in 1821.

Sorghum molasses is made at French Camp every Saturday in late September and October.

French Camp

Cotton, which was the South's major crop for many years, is still grown along the Trace.

Autumn on the Trace

Jeff Busby Park overlook is on one of the highest points in Mississippi (603 feet). The park is named for the Mississippi Congressman who introduced legislation creating the Natchez Trace Parkway.

South of Tupelo, near Jeff Busby Park

Chuquatonchee Creek near the site of the old Chickasaw Agency

Barn near Tupelo

Hornet's nest

South of Tupelo

Brice's Cross Roads, site of a Confederate attack led by Generals Stephen D. Lee and Nathan Bedford Forrest

Construction on the Tennessee-Tombigbee, a 234-mile waterway, authorized by the U. S. Congress in 1946, begun in 1972, completed in 1985.

South of Iuka

Farmland, privately owned and much of it under cultivation, borders the Trace.

Buzzard Roost spring, in Alabama, site of Chickasaw Chief Levi Colbert's stand

Bridge over the Tennessee River, which early travelers crossed by the ferry operated by George Colbert, powerful Chickasaw chief

Tennessee homestead near Alabama state line

Approaching Sweetwater Branch nature trail, Tennessee

On Sweetwater Branch nature trail

Metal Ford, Tennessee, where early travelers forded the Buffalo River, was the site of an early iron industry.

Old Trace Drive in Tennessee follows over two and one-half miles of the original Trace route.

Napier Mine in Tennessee was worked for iron ore in the 19th century

A park and burial site commemorates Captain Meriwether Lewis of Lewis and Clark fame, who met his death on the Trace in 1809.

In Meriwether Lewis Park, Tennessee

Tobacco farm and drying shed along the Trace in Tennessee

Tennessee tobacco farm

Old Trace Walk, near the end of the Trace in Tennessee

Hay field near Tennessee River

Once over the Duck River in Tennessee, the early traveler was hiking through the rolling hills leading to Nashville.

Near the northern end of the unfinished Trace, Shady Grove, Tennessee

Passing through Columbia, Tennessee, the traveler can visit the home of President James K. Polk. The house is now a museum with many of the original furnishings.

At the northern terminus of the Trace today, the traveler must take U.S. Highway 50 through Columbia, Tennessee, to get to Nashville. Six miles south of Columbia is St. John's Episcopal Church where Confederate General Leonidas Polk served as the first rector.

Site of Fort Negley where the Battle of Nashville began in 1864.

Near Nashville, the destination of northbound travelers on the Trace, Andrew Jackson built his home, the Hermitage. The original house burned and Jackson rebuilt this structure in 1834. He died there in 1845.

The northern end of the Trace